Contents

W9-CXO-051

Credits, Contributors, and Co-Conspirators

Resource List

MINDFUL OCCUPATION:

Rising Up Without Burning Out

Printed in U.S.-occupied America

This guide is written in the spirit of mutual aid and peer support.

This is a living document! We encourage you to remix this material to suit your own local needs. There are important, relevant ideas absent from this booklet because of space, time, and our own limited perspectives. Please join the conversation online, in your communities, and within yourself.

First Edition, June 2012
ISBN-13: 978-0-9858208-0-0
ISBN: 0985820802

Mindful Occupation
c/o RVA Icarus, P.O. Box 7019, Richmond, VA 23221
info@mindfuloccupation.org

You can also download a digital version of this guide at **mindfuloccupation.org**.

Please send corrections and typos to **errata@mindfuloccupation.org**.

A society that is increasingly socially fragmented and divided, where the gulf between success and failure seems so large, where the only option open to many is highly demanding and low paid work, where the only cheap and simple route to carelessness is through drugs, is likely to make people particularly vulnerable to mental disintegration in its many forms.

Joanna Moncrief, MD

Try to remember that taking care of ourselves in the emotional and physical sense is a revolutionary act. The world can be a really sick place, and we need to care for ourselves in ways we were never taught we'd have to.

Kim Christoffel

Human salvation lies in the hands of the creatively maladjusted.

Martin Luther King, Jr.

Introduction

You Are Not Alone

Welcome!

What you hold in your hands is a rough toolkit of ideas and visions. It is meant to be shared, discussed and used for action as the Occupy* movement evolves. This booklet is the result of a bunch of dedicated people working together, friends and strangers, online and in person, in living rooms and out in the streets, all across North America.

The folks who put together this booklet come from different backgrounds, all involved with on-the-ground Occupy protests in various cities and towns. Many of us have been working on issues of radical mental health and activism for quite some time, involved with groups such as the Icarus Project, MindFreedom International, and the Freedom Center. Others are mental health professionals and street medics who have been involved in supporting the Occupy protesters on the ground. What binds us together is respect for each other's personal experiences, and our commitment to community-based approaches to emotional support.

We are all passionate folks who care about the people in our movement. We know that involvement in activism can make people, including ourselves, especially prone to highs and lows. Sometimes we feel incredible, knowing we are part of shaping history in the streets with our friends, and other times we may find ourselves desperate and burnt out, feeling the entire world suffering under our solitary skin. In creating this booklet, we aim to address the need for attention to mental health, healing, and emotional first aid within Occupy groups.

Occupy is an evolving movement, affected by the forces of passion, time, police, government, corporations, tactics, weather, creativity, and the growing pains that all activist movements experience. Some suggestions in this booklet are about making sustainable encampments, many of which have been temporarily destroyed by the police and government. Other suggestions are applicable for any and all activist groups working on making social change. Still other suggestions are

* We have decided to use the term "Occupy" because it reflects the current language of the movement. However, we recognize that this word can seem to both reenact and erase violent histories of colonization and imperialism. We find other terms less problematic and more useful (e.g., "Decolonize", "Liberate", or "Unoccupy.")

general helpful ideas for taking care of ourselves and others as we live our lives.

We envision a vibrant movement made up of locally based community groups and professionals in the field, a movement that understands the importance of language and telling stories and knowing our history, a movement that has reverence for the human spirit and understands the intertwined complexity of these things we call mental health and wellness. We understand the importance of economic justice, diversity and global solidarity. We see the critical need for accepting, even celebrating, mental diversity, while evading the trap of fitting into a society that is obviously very sick. Fundamentally, we recognize an urgency: if we are going to shift the current paradigm, we need a movement that has both the political savvy to understand how to fight the system, and the tools to take care of each other as the world gets even crazier.

There is an urgent need to talk publicly about the relationship between social injustice and our mental health. We need to start redefining what it actually means to be mentally healthy, not just on an individual level, but on collective, communal, and global levels.

The Strength of Our Collective Hearts

Our psyches, souls, and hearts contribute to collective social change in unique and important ways. We need to create a space for them to speak, and be heard, in the communities in which we work. It's important to remember that we don't have to always show our "strong" selves; we are trying to create a world in which "weakness," emotion, and vulnerability are not seen as problems. To be strong, we should be able to feel the full range of emotions, not just keep them bottled up inside. This is extremely important when it comes to activism, because we are much stronger as a community if we allow this full range in one another. If we deny our feelings, or hold them in until they explode out in unhealthy ways, we are more likely to burn out, or to bring other people down in the process. We also risk ignoring what our bodies are telling us about our selves, each other, and what's going on around us.

This booklet offers some useful ideas to strengthen our psychic, soulful, and heartfelt contributions to making the world a more nourishing place. Some of the writings and art here have been previously published in different form, and some of it was created within days of going to press. All of it was written in the spirit of mutual aid and cooperation. Let's take really good care of each other out there!

Mad Love!

Through working together—all of us in our different ways of psyche, soul, and heart—we move toward real solidarity!

Bexa

What Is Radical Mental Health?

Stories matter. Many stories matter. Stories have been used to dispossess and to malign. But, stories can also be used to empower and to humanize. Stories can break the dignity of a people, but stories can also repair that dignity.
Chimamanda Adiche

Radical mental health means conceiving of, and engaging with, "mental health" and "mental illness" from a new perspective. There are many ways to understand our psychic states, flows, and differences, and there is a rich tradition of groups and individuals that have been exploring the boundaries of these experiences for many years. What follows is a list of key principles that we find woven through this diverse movement; it is not intended to be exhaustive or universal, but more to offer an overall sense of who we are, what we do, and why.

Radical mental health is about the grass roots and diversity. For so long, our psychic differences have been defined by authority figures intent on fitting us into narrow versions of "normality." Radical mental health is a dynamic, creative term; one which empowers us to come up with our own understandings for how our psyches, souls, and hearts experience the world, rather than pour them into conventional medical frameworks. For example, the Icarus Project understands people's capacities for altered states as, "dangerous gifts" to be cultivated and taken care of, rather than a disease or disorder to be cured or eliminated. Indeed, by joining together as a community, they believe that, "the intertwined threads of madness and creativity can inspire hope and transformation in a repressed and damaged world." It follows that any realistic approach to well-being has to begin by accepting and valuing diversity. There is no single model for a "healthy mind," no matter how many years of drug treatment, schooling, or behavior modification programs we've been put through. And without differences, there can be no movement.

Radical mental health is about interconnectedness. While mainstream conceptions of mental health and illness reduce people's experiences into brain chemicals or personal histories, radical mental health sees human experience as a holistic convergence of social, emotional, cultural, physical, spiritual, historical, and environmental elements. This interconnectedness also spirals outwards with the idea that we all share this planet together—humans, animals, insects, and plants— what happens in one world affects all other worlds. We don't have to see ourselves as separate beings, but rather in terms of relationships: a part of myself "overlaps" with a part of you; if you're hurt I can be hurt too. No matter how alienated we are by the world around us, no matter how out of step, depressed, and disconnected we might feel, We Are Not Alone. Our lives are supported by the lives of countless other beings, from the microbes in our eyelashes to the people who plant our strawberries. The world is so much more complicated and beautiful than it appears on the surface. A premise of radical mental health then, is not only that we are not left to deal with everything on our own, but that things that support our well-being can come in many different forms (they do not just have to be psychological or pharmaceutical).

The growth and strength of individuals and communities comes from our interconnectedness—we struggle and celebrate together, always.

Radical mental health is about emotional/embodied expertise. Although careful to not overly romanticize suffering or different mental states (obviously, some can be very painful and disruptive, or even fatal) we see the beauty and expertise in all of our feelings. Radical mental health is about survival—not "survival of the fittest" or survival through teeth-gritting, but survival through chaos and exploration. It means observing how others support themselves— things which might seem self-destructive from afar—with compassion and understanding. Radical mental health is about opening up doors for conversation; about taking shame out of the equation. It is not about trying to fit into narrow definitions of "normal," which are always wrong anyway, because every culture, every group, every place might have its own normal. Radical mental health is about using your lifetime to learn about yourself, your loved ones, and strangers too, and envisioning and moving towards NORM societies and ways of living which better support us all. It is about making worlds that recognize "breaking down" as a meaningful, important part of life that must be attended to, tended, and not necessarily fended off. Radical mental health is about listening to and learning from the expertise of our feelings and bodies.

Radical mental health is about new languages and cultures. Language is powerful. It can open the world up like sunrise and it can block out the sky like prison walls. We have other people's language in our heads and on our tongues. The medical authorities offer us all kinds of words to talk about ourselves and the troubles we have, like "depression" and "psychosis." Sometimes these words help us look back on our lives with a new way of understanding what was going on, but too often these words end up putting us in sad, separate boxes where we feel like there's something wrong with us and we can't connect to anyone else. Words like "disorder" and "disease" offer us one set of metaphors for understanding the way we experience our lives through our unique minds and souls, but it is such a limited view. We think in language, constantly filtering all our perceptions through the available structures of words and metaphors in our brain—in many senses the available metaphors create our reality. If we can change the metaphors that shape our minds, we can change the reality around us. We need to get together and find language for our stories that make sense to us; to unlearn social conditioning about what it means to be "sick" and "healthy." We should feel empowered to create words that better reflect our personal experiences. Some of us have reclaimed the term "mad" or "madness" as no longer negative, but rather, as a proud statement of survival.

Radical mental health is about challenging the dominance of biopsychiatry. The biomedical model of psychiatry, or "biopsychiatry," rests on the belief that mental health issues are the result of chemical imbalances in the brain. It is an idea that is wrapped up in the same ideology of the marketplace that has cut our social safety nets and fragmented our communities—that is, that the problems and solutions of our lives are located solely in the individual. More and more, the belief that our dis/ease is in our brains has desensitized us to the idea that our feelings and experiences often have their roots in social and political issues. If we are going to do anything to change the mental health system (along with the decaying economic system!) we need to begin by simply acknowledging how fundamentally flawed the current, medicalized model is—how it privileges "specialists," "professionals," and "scientists" in such a way that can undermine the expertise of personal experiences, local communities, and alternative models of well-being. In addition, a clearer distinction must be drawn between the usefulness of some modern psychiatric drugs for some people at some times, and the biopsychiatric program that shrinks our minds into brains, and our feelings into chemical reactions. Above all, radical mental health urges us to talk publicly about the relationship between social and economic injustice, the pharmaceutical industry, and our psychic well-being. As such, it is about redefining what it actually means to be "mentally healthy" not just on an individual level, but on community and global levels.

Radical mental health is about options. Some may assume that radical mental health is simply "anti-psychiatry." However, most of us take far more complicated, diverse, and nuanced viewpoints. Radical mental health may mean accepting some of the things that mainstream, medicalized models suggest for our well-being, while discarding some of the things we may not find useful, helpful, or positive. In practice, this means supporting people's self-determination for personal, ongoing decision-making, including whether to take psychiatric drugs or not, and whether to use diagnostic categories or not. Importantly, this support is done with an acknowledgement that the pressure to make more medicalized choices is significant in our society and that these carry considerably more influence than (and often shout over) alternatives. In addition, while medical tools may sometimes be useful in the short term, some diagnoses turn our experiences into chronic incurable sickness, and its treatments come with their own problems that cannot be ignored. Radical mental health, then, often includes taking a "harm reduction" approach (promoting strategies to reduce harmful consequences) with regard to people's use of psychiatric diagnoses and drugs. Radical alternatives to mainstream approaches celebrate multiple options and diverse forms of expertise. They value, for example, peer support, listening, dialogue, mutual aid, activism, counseling, spirituality, creative activity, community engagement, politicization, and access to more marginalized healing methods.

Radical mental health is about politics and social justice. Radical mental health understands how the tools of psychiatric intervention are embedded in broader relations of power. People in power benefit from controlling and silencing how our psyches/bodies/souls speak about an unjust world. They also see these tools as part of a powerful, global medico-industrial complex that profits from framing our experiences as chronic illnesses that require lifelong treatment. Participating in radical mental health activism might include denouncing how the pharmaceutical industry gains from creating new diagnostic categories, and agitating on major scales for changes among mental health institutions, professionals, government policies, and insurance companies. A radical mental health lens could also mean looking at the history of psychology with a skeptical eye; researching how definitions of madness vary across time and space, and as such are socially produced and have political (as well as personal) consequences. For example, the psychiatric establishment has a history of diagnosing entire groups of people who were queer, black, women, poor, gender-variant and/or trans, sick and abnormal, therefore justifying forms of violence and exclusion that maintained the dominance of whiteness, patriarchy, and heternormativity.

Radical mental health then, is about returning the pathologizing gaze to our crazy-making world. Our struggles for mad justice intersect with others challenging oppressive social relations, including anti-racist, feminist, queer, decolonization, disability, antiwar, decarceration, anti-corporate, public education, and other grassroots community movements.

Radical mental health is about questioning and imagination. Radical mental health questions authorities and critiques accepted knowledge. It draws attention to the ways that diagnostic categories and treatment regimes can be based on assumptions about science and expertise that deny the subjective and political nature of all knowledges, especially those that are embedded in powerful social and corporate structures that have a vested interest in pushing illness models of madness. Radical mental health, then, might mean critiquing some of the assumptions underpinning mainstream approaches to our psyches. For example, the concept that being a "productive member of society" means the production of certain goods, or performing certain types of jobs, even though these may serve our unjust economic structure, over individual or community well-being.

QUESTION!

In addition, radical mental health is about imagining what could be. Our psychic experiences are seen as an important source of desire and possibility; a (sometimes distressing, sometimes delightful) place of learning and revolution that can be squashed or hardened when approached solely through a medical lens of fear, risk, or danger.

We need to reclaim our dreams and scheme up ways to make them happen. We need to share everything we've figured out about how to be a human being. We need to love ourselves as we are—crooked and intense, powerful and frightening, unruly and prone to mess around in the dirt—and understand that weeds are simply plants who refuse to be domesticated and displayed. We need to write new maps of the universes we share in common and find ways to heal together.

Radical mental health is about working within, and without, the bigger mental health systems. Radical mental health activists have a diversity of perspectives towards hospitalization, medication, and diagnoses. Most of us are not dogmatic about these issues, although we make a critical distinction between an individual's informed consent and a critique of the psychiatric establishment and the pharmaceutical industry. One of the most radical aspects of radical mental health has to do with questioning authority and the production of knowledge. We challenge the exclusive voice of formal expertise, and demand that our stories and experiences be considered alongside the voices of professional mental health service providers, profiteers, and institutions. Along with the disability rights movement, we insist: **Nothing about us without us.**

We recognize that there are many people who work in mainstream mental health settings who are deeply committed to anti-oppressive practices, who are end users of mental health care, who are traumatized by working in profoundly unjust and under-resourced systems, and who aim to share hope and support with the people most victimized by those systems. As such, while being in some ways "cogs" in a highly flawed system, they (we) are also allies in any systemic change. We need each other. For radical shifts to a monstrous, complex structure can only occur through dialogue and movement across multiple forms, people, and sites.

Dandelion Roots

There are so many of us out here who feel the world with thin skin and heavy hearts, who get called crazy because we're too full of fire and pain, who know that other worlds exist and aren't comfortable in this version of reality. We've been busting up out of sidewalks and blooming all kind of misfit flowers for as long as people have been walking on this Earth.

So many of us have access to secret layers of consciousness — you could think of us like dandelion roots that gather minerals from hidden layers of the soil that other plants don't reach. If we're lucky, we share them with everyone on the surface—because we feel things stronger than the other people around us, a lot of us have visions about how things could be different, why they need to be different, and it's painful to keep them silent. Sometimes we get called sick, and sometimes we get called sacred, but no matter how they name us, we are a vital part of making this planet whole.

It's time we connect our underground roots and tell our buried stories, grow up strong and scatter our visions all over the patches of scarred and damaged soil in a society that is so desperately in need of change.

Connecting Radical Mental Health and Occupy

Ira Birch

Corporate (In)Justice

I t's easy to see connections between radical mental health and the Occupy movement. After all, both movements are challenging the objectification of persons and nature at large. In the radical mental health movement, we raise our voices against the mainstream mental health system in which our complex experiences are objectified into labels that fit cookie-cutter understandings of mental health. In the Occupy movement, we raise our voices against the corporate-centered culture where our lives are treated as objects whose purpose is to bring financial gain to corporations.

The injustice in the mental health system closely intertwines with the injustice that results from corporatocracy. To begin with, our mental distress is always inseparable from the socioeconomic circumstances that we are in. Further, pharmaceutical corporations exploit our insecurities as an opportunity for revenue growth. In addition to advertising drugs as an effective tool to fix a "chemical imbalance," corporate influence corrupts the powers that be in the mental health system. Time and again we find out about financial ties between pharmaceutical companies, researchers, and members of the working groups for the Diagnostic and Statistical Manual of Mental Disorders (DSM) that is used to categorize and pathologize our psyches. Moreover, the government does little to regulate corporate greed, as the Food and Drug Administration (FDA) relies on research conducted by the pharmaceutical corporations when approving new drugs. These corporations are driven to maximize shareholder value, rather than follow the Hippocratic Oath to "do no harm."

When corporations that prioritize productivity over community are culturally and politically sanctified, challenging the status quo seems all the more difficult. However, through social protest—whether with Occupy or radical mental health—we take a step against the accepted paradigm to reclaim our humanity and community. Given that we are putting our real selves on the line, we may become stressed. We may be hurt. We may be traumatized. That is why it is important to learn how to give and take care of ourselves, through mutual support and community. It's fundamentally important to try to match our process in doing this work with the product that we are collectively seeking.

(Un)Occupying Violence

The Occupy movement weaves together the struggles of communities who refuse to go on carrying the burdens of an unjust economic structure; burdens that land especially in bodies that are poor, of color, female, queer, trans, and/or differently abled.

And burdens that can manifest as madness.

M. Osborn

Yet, backed by a medico-industrial complex that profits from turning injustice into sickness, these mad expressions are framed as an individual's "mental illness," diverting critical attention from our crazy-making world. Such mainstream approaches are therefore both product and tool of imperialism, capitalism, neoliberalism, and securitization; those very systems that many within Occupy are striving to undo.

It follows that madness connects deeply with Occupy. Yet, conflated with aggression, it is instead increasingly seen as a threat that needs to be screened out or eliminated. Such an approach ignores that the vast majority of madness is not violent (in fact, madness is much more affiliated with surviving violence) and that the vast majority of violence is considered "rational" (the violent actions of the state, corporations, white supremacy, and patriarchy, for example). In addition, sentiments within Occupy that criminalize and scapegoat "the crazies" often primarily target participants who are homeless and/or people of color. These racist and classist assumptions distract from the ever-present threat of police brutality and depict Occupy as divided and unstable to "the outside."

As a site of solidarity, violence of all kinds is clearly not okay within Occupy; there needs to be a process of accountability for harmful words and actions. However, violence does not have to be diagnosed as "mental illness," and would benefit from being addressed in consultation with the communities who are being blamed.

We are working hard to create a space within Occupy for diverse connections, particularly as mad voices disproportionately represent bodies already marginalized and policed by society. We have been organizing for mad justice, and offering social and emotional support on site to all protesters—no matter what form their protest takes—through written materials, teach-ins, counseling, peer support, medic training, and community building.

Using a lens of diversity, protest, and community, radical psych sees madness as containing seeds of expertise, imagination, and change. It offers learning and growth to Occupy and deserves to be actively included (not just tolerated) in "the 99 percent." For we all desire, require revolution.

Taking Care of the Basics

Nourishing Mind/Body/Soul/Each Other

Protest is physically, emotionally, spiritually, socially, and politically intense. Even moment to moment, it can shift from being exceptionally enriching and energizing to exasperating and exhausting. One of the most effective ways to deal with these desires and disruptions is to establish and sustain a collective, holistic space that nourishes people's individual needs as important, unique elements of a dedicated, diverse, and active community. Below are some ideas:

♥ SCHEDULE: Schedules can reduce mind clutter and stress, creating more space for engaging in activities with depth and calmness. If you're here to participate in particular actions, a schedule can help you feel more prepared, secure, and confident.

♥ SLEEP: If and when things go down, being well rested will give you a better chance of being resilient. Seven hours of sleep vs. two really can make all the difference. Think about what you need to sleep soundly (warm clothing, blankets, earplugs, eye cover, sleep aids, etc.), and share these with each other. Collectively take shifts to ensure that you are all individually nourished.

♥ EAT & DRINK: Stay hydrated, eat as well as you can, and keep your blood sugar up (low sugar, no/limited caffeine). Sharing meals together is a great way to build friendships and community.

♥ SUPPORT: Build and stay connected to your own unique, creative support system of healing and inspiring people, things, spaces, and activities—both nearby and farther away. Support each other to take the time out to do this; nurturing individual needs contributes positively to the collective.

♥ HERBS & MEDS: Keep up with any herbal or medication regimens you may be on. Keep your prescription bottle on you, ID, and preferably a note from your doctor. This will increase your chances of getting to take your meds if you are arrested.

♥ STAY EMBODIED: Your body is a significant site for processing (potential) stress and trauma. Take care of it, listen to it, and nourish it with touch and movement. Stretch; massage your shoulders, hands, feet, and/or face; take slow, deep breaths; notice the tension in your body, and let it go as you exhale. For some people, embodiment may also mean trying to avoid excessive alcohol and drugs. While people will make these decisions for themselves, it is important to recognize that intoxication can negatively affect protests by disrupting our connections with our bodies and each other.

♥ PLAY: Part of decompressing and dealing with trauma is remaining alive. In addition to dealing with the serious matters at hand, it helps to have fun. Done with sensitivity, laughter is a shiny way to heal, gain perspective, and connect with one another. Building a spirit of playfulness, poetics, and performance into your space and actions also supports sustainability and solidarity.

♥ TALK AND LISTEN: Being prepared before things get hectic can be helpful. Talk with people about what's difficult for you and what helps you when things get rough. Actively create a supportive space for others to do the same. This kind of communication happens on multiple levels. Stay tuned in to each other, listen, reflect, and ask questions. We can all learn and grow from each others' experiences.

♥ SPACE: We are not separate from our physical surroundings. Thoughtfully building this space will help to calm, cleanse, and invigorate your emotional well-being and promote a sense of inclusion and community. Collectively making a space is also a great way to build connections, begin conversations about our overlapping and diverse needs and aspirations, and get creative!

♥ CONNECT: It is important to realize that you are not alone. Take time to build friendships with your fellow protesters and support each other. Draw connections between what you are experiencing on a personal level and the big picture—experiences of your fellow protesters, broader Occupy movements, everyday injustices lived by diverse communities, struggles for resistance and change by other groups across time and place, nature and the Earth, spiritual exploration, global revolution—you name it!

Basic Tips for Sustainable "Occupy" Street Protests

Form an AFFINITY GROUP—a group of friends to protest with. Swap names, phone numbers, and emergency contacts. Keep together and plan what you're likely to do if confronted by the police, keeping in mind that some people in your group may be more susceptible to police harassment, brutality, and arrest (e.g., people of color, and trans folk.) It can be a challenge to stick with a big group, so also consider having a "Protest Buddy"—one person that you march/action with. Afterwards, check in and debrief with the whole group; reflecting on your experiences, and offering each other social and emotional support.

The biggest risk with a sustained protest outside in cold weather is HYPOTHERMIA. Stay dry (always carry a rain poncho), eat, drink (always carry a bottle of water), and rest. Make sure you dress in layers: next to your skin wear thin synthetic (not cotton) material, then add something thin and warm, followed by a thick layer like wool or fleece, and finally a wind/waterproof layer, a hat, and mittens. If clothes get wet, change; and if you become too hot, remove some layers (it's better not to sweat). For really cold days, put a small amount of cayenne pepper in your shoes (not in your socks), or use heat mits. As a group you should also try to find a nearby location in which people can warm up. To stay warm while sleeping: wear dry clothes, have extra socks, keep your bedding dry and off the ground, close all tent entrances, and try and source an electric lamp as this will also give off heat. Finally, keep an eye out for signs of severe hypothermia—if you or someone else has stopped shivering, is cold, has blue or puffy skin, are mumbling, and/or stumbling, get help! (Check out the "Occupy Winter" group on Facebook for more tips on dealing with the cold.)

RESPECT that many people are involved here. (Yay!) Some are seasoned activists, others are brand new. Some of us are very conscious of things like sexism, racism, homophobia, transphobia, classism, and abelism and will notice these "isms" even in the protests. Be PATIENT with each other. People aren't usually trying to be bigots—they're just new to understanding how these insidious oppressive ideas take root in us and how we all perpetuate them to some degree. Assess the situation. Seek out support and SPEAK UP in a manner you feel comfortable with if you feel someone's causing harm. "Safer Spaces" groups and other groups in various Occupy encampments will be working on ways to make it easier to address these issues. Try to stay calm and LISTEN to one another—we all have a lot to learn from people who are historically marginalized.

Respect your INTUITION and your BOUNDARIES. Just because someone is in the same protest doesn't mean they're necessarily a safe person to hang out with; you have to feel that out for yourself, and may want to show up initially with a good, trusted friend. Also be mindful about what you need to do to take care of yourself. We all have roles to play, and some may find that certain actions are not for them. Sleeping outside, for instance, day in and day out, in cramped spaces filled with people, can be very hard on our physical and emotional selves. For example, to take care of our mental health one of the most important things is to get enough sleep, but the encampments can make that hard—while you could use earplugs, you then won't be as safe when it comes to dealing with possible police problems. Or maybe you're in a situation in your life where you absolutely can't risk getting arrested, so you have to make strategic choices about which activities to engage in. It's important to know that there's many ways to participate in these movements—contributing what you can, when you can, is wonderful. One of the beautiful things about being involved in protests as a diverse collective (rather than as an individual) is being able to create a space where people can step forward or back as they need to, without feeling like they are carrying the full responsibility of the movement on their shoulders. We are in this together.

Avoiding ARREST isn't always possible because the production of fear, panic, and aggression, is a key tactic used by police to undermine protesters and protests. However, we can keep our collective ears out for clues of impending arrest situations: Police will be more tense and coordinated. Pay attention to their radios and bullhorns, discretely listen in on conversations, and be aware of shift changes. In addition, consider how police have been treating the protests in general—if they have been arresting people at random during marches that don't have permits and you can't risk arrest, then consider sitting these ones out and/or supporting the action in other ways (like writing letters of support to the newspaper or calling political officials). If you are arrested, stay calm. If you have important medications that you need, demand them repeatedly; you may also request to go to a hospital. You also have a right to a sandwich. Make a note of officer badge numbers and names. Make sure you have the LEGAL SUPPORT phone number written on your body. Also have some spare quarters, and call them as soon as you can.

Police BRUTALITY during an action and/or arrest poses another significant risk to our emotional, social, and physical well-being— particularly for folks who are brown, black, and/or trans and therefore more likely to be targeted for violence. Stand up for/with each other— name and shame attacks that are blatantly racist, sexist, or homophobic. In a possible arrest situation or march, take off earrings or other dangly jewelry, tuck long hair away, keep scarves and other clothing close to your body, and try not to have a bag with a long strap—all of these may get pulled and lead to added harm. Yell "MEDIC!" if you or someone else is hurt. (Street medics are trained in basic medical procedures to help protesters; they wear red crosses on their clothes.)

Notice if police are carrying a big canister that looks kind of like a fire extinguisher—this may be PEPPER SPRAY (they may also have it in pellets, foam, or small cans). It will burn your eyes and skin like crazy, and can make you nauseous. If you get sprayed, try to take your contacts out (for this reason it is actually best to avoid wearing them at all during actions). Don't rub your eyes; instead OPEN THEM AND CRY. Wash them out with LAW (liquid antacid—Maalox—and water). Tip your head to the side and start from the inner eye so that it runs across and out the other side.

Look out for police in riot gear with gas masks—some may be holding huge TEARGAS guns that they use to shoot out teargas canisters. If you have asthma, other breathing issues, or are pregnant, try to get out. If possible walk to higher ground as teargas will sink to lower areas. (General protest etiquette is to not run because people can be trampled, but in extreme situations, you might consider it as a way to care for yourself.) Teargas makes you feel blind and like you can't breathe for about five to twenty minutes. It can also have long-term physical effects, but mostly it can be an extremely TRIGGERING experience for many. It is loud and scary. It is possible to hold your ground, too, though often police use the teargas as a way of clearing an area, storming in like a line of robots. Be aware that the teargas canisters are extremely hot and can burn you if you try to pick them up without heat-safe gloves. One way to protect yourself is by wearing plastic goggles (like tight-fitting swim goggles) with a respirator. For a more low-tech option, cover your mouth and nose with a water-soaked rag and close your eyes. Teargas is not as effective when there's water, and cider vinegar in the water on the rag can also help. Breathe through your nose, not your mouth. Afterward, wash your face in COLD water and castille soap. Later, take a cool shower and wash your clothes, as they will continue to give off gas.

Assume UNDERCOVER police are around. They may act as provocateurs, or just be spying on you. Don't out anyone's name or other info without their consent.

Collectively DEBRIEF after difficult situations. Some Occupy areas have set up "Emotional First Aid" tents where you can talk, rest, or engage in other types of healing. Sometimes it's also a good idea to connect with people who are far removed from the action, as people who are on the scene themselves may also become traumatized. You may want to take some time away from the protests to revive yourself.

BE PROUD! You're joining a historic and transnational legacy of strong, effective struggles for resistance that make injustices visible and intolerable, pushing us towards a better reality. Remember that Occupy is a site of protest, and of possibility. Work together to incorporate politicized playfulness and creative performances into your protests. An atmosphere of fear, aggression, and competition is not sustainable for our psyches, souls, or communities; an atmosphere of desire, vibrancy, and connectivity, is.

Erik Ruin

Taking Care of the Basics

Coping Skills in Times of Stress

What Is Stress?

Stress is simply your body's response to change. Since your environment is constantly changing, you are constantly under some level of stress. Your nervous system is equipped to handle a certain "normal" level of stress. This "normal" level of stress, or the amount of stress that a given person can experience without experiencing the physical symptoms of stress, varies from person to person.

When you have surpassed the normal level of stress that your body is equipped to handle, you will begin to experience the physical and emotional effects of stress, and your behavior will change as well.

What Are Stressors?

A stressor is defined as any physical, psychological, or social force that puts real or perceived demands on the body, emotions, mind, or spirit of an individual. Simply put, a stressor is something that causes stress.

What Are Coping Skills (Strategies)?

We all develop defense mechanisms to avoid or lessen psychological pain. Coping skills are ways in which we learn to deal with various stressors. Each person copes with stress differently. Over time, we all construct coping strategies that are "right" for us as thinking and feeling individuals. "Right" is in quotes because many people often do not realize that how they deal with life stressors is not only unhelpful, but also destructive, negative, and painful for not only themselves but those around them.

Coping strategies can be both constructive/adaptive or destructive/ maladaptive. Maladaptive coping skills are ways of dealing with stress that usually make things worse. These types of coping strategies can hurt your social relationships, make preexisting problems worse, and even result in new symptoms of a stress-related injury. Many of us have known someone who has overreacted to something which resulted in them losing touch with a friend or loved one. Maladaptive coping strategies put pressure on your relationships with friends, family, comrades, and coworkers. They can damage your body or create more emotional pain in the long term, even when they seem helpful in the short term. In extreme cases, maladaptive coping skills can ruin lives. Through the information in this booklet, and psychological activism, we can lessen the impact of negativity in our lives, including that which we inflict on ourselves through learned maladaptive coping skills.

Allow Yourself to Feel

"If I don't think about it, it's not there, right?"

Some people believe that it is best not to think about a troublesome issue, thought, or feeling, as getting upset about it may only make the issue worse. In some instances, this will be true, depending on how you react to any given situation. However, we must never put a troubling issue to the back of our minds in hopes that time will make it all go away. Such behavior is often harmful in the long run. Sure, you will not be "bothered" by such thoughts right this moment, but while you're ignoring your problems THEY ARE STILL PRESENT IN YOUR AND OTHERS'LIVES. What is most beneficial for all involved (especially your own long-term mental health!) is to deal with any stress, anxiety, or troubling issue as it arises. Waiting for time to "take its course" in solving your problems may create more stress in your life.

In many cases of maladaptive coping, we do not allow ourselves to feel and analyze our emotions. You should always ALLOW YOURSELF TO FEEL. Often, our rational self tells us that feeling isn't constructive. Socializing in our society has conditioned us to believe this. This is true for all people, although society socializes genders differently. Regardless of your gender, FEELING IS NORMAL. Allowing yourself to feel a whole range of emotions about any given situation is healthy. What you do in reaction to these emotions, however, can be unhealthy.

Leaving the Situation When "Fight or Flight" Kicks In

The first step when confronted with a stressful situation is to remove yourself physically from the stressor. Doing this will give you time away from the stressor to process how you feel. If you remain in physical proximity to something that causes you stress, you will not have the mental capacity to focus on your thoughts. If the stressor is a person and you do not take a physical time out, you may lash out irrationally at them, whether verbally or physically. I keep emphasizing "physical" because at no point should you distance yourself emotionally. If you are engaged in a conversation and want to continue the conversation once you cool off, consider saying, "I need to take a time out. Can we continue the conversation in 30 minutes?"

Once you are away from the stressor, take some deep breaths, sit down, and allow yourself to feel. If you are angry, be angry. If you are sad, feel free to cry. Feel whatever feelings come to you—do not suppress them. Try writing about it, or talking to someone who is far-removed from the situation. Make sure you allow yourself 20 minutes to calm down. This is not just an arbitrary number. It takes the body 20 minutes to get out of "fight or flight" mode.

Coping with Overwhelming Emotions (A Quick Reference List)

A common reaction to experiencing overwhelming emotions is a heightened sense of personal vulnerability or fear. The following strategies may lessen the impact overwhelming emotions will have on your mental health.

♥ Validate the emotion. Remind yourself that it is normal to experience feeling overwhelmed as well as the range of other emotions you may be experiencing.

♥ Share your emotions with others. Understanding, supportive others who can listen to you often provide relief. You may find that they have experienced similar overwhelming emotions sometime in their life. Even if you do not talk about your emotions, the company of supportive others who are experiencing similar reactions, thoughts, and feelings can be a comfort.

♥ If you do not want to be alone, find ways to be with others. Spending time with familiar others can make you feel safer and more comfortable. Entertain the notion of inviting a friend over to spend the night with you, travel across town with friends, and let people know you would like their company.

♥ Create a safe environment. Analyze your living, working, and school environment and identify ways to increase your sense of personal safety and security.

♥ Obtain accurate information about your reactions. Seek out the assistance of informed others who can help you sort out your feelings and thoughts. Avoid persons who deny or minimize your experience.

♥ Realize that you cannot control everything. Often our fears are exacerbated by situations that remind us that we cannot control all persons, places, and things. It is often helpful to identify those things that are in our control, and to try to let go of those things that are not.

♥ Remember that your emotions are valid. Over time, you will start to regain your sense of security and balance. If you feel that you could benefit from assistance in this process, seek out a peer support group or mental health professional. It is often helpful to consult with others in a therapeutic setting if you feel that your daily functioning is negatively affected. "Therapeutic" does not have to equal "professional"! Stick with what makes you feel comfortable.

Mindful Communication with Others

Mindful communication is often the key to a successful relationship. If you're constantly making judgmental statements to someone, the chances are good that you'll lose that relationship. Let's look at how to be more mindful of the messages you send to other people.

Consider the following statements:

"You make me mad."

"You're such a jerk, I could scream."

"Sometimes you make me so upset I just want to end it all."

"I know that you did that to me on purpose just to hurt me."

What do all of these statements have in common? It's true that they all express some kind of emotion, such as anger, distress, and sadness. But more importantly, they're all judgments of the other person. Each of the statements blames the other person for the way the speaker feels. Now consider how you would feel if someone said one of these statements to you. What would you do? Maybe you would say something just as angry back to the person, which would lead to a big fight. The result would be that nothing gets resolved. Judgmental statements like these stop any form of effective communication. So what can you do instead?

One of the solutions is to turn "you" statements into mindful "I" statements. Mindful "I" statements:

▼ Are based on your own mindful awareness of how you feel.

▼ Are a more accurate description of how you feel.

▼ Let a person know how you feel in a nonjudgmental way.

▼ Evoke greater empathy and understanding from the other person, which allows the person to meet your needs.

Turn Judgmental "You" Statements into Mindful "I" Statements

Here are several judgmental "you" statements turned into mindful "I" statements. After looking over these examples, take the opportunity to write down your own.

Judgmental "You" Statement	Mindful "I" Statement
"You make me feel horrible."	"It makes me feel really horrible when you use negative name-calling."
"I know you're doing this on purpose to make me go crazy."	"I sometimes feel unsure of your intentions behind some of the things you do or say. Because of this unsurity, I sometimes come to the conclusion that you are purposefully trying to hurt me."
"You're being insulting."	"I feel insulted when you say that/take that tone with me/roll your eyes at me."
"Stop fooling around; you're getting on my nerves."	"I feel anxious/tired/angry/annoyed when you tease me like that."
"If you don't listen to what I'm telling you, I'm not going to talk to you anymore."	"I feel like my thoughts and feelings are not being heard. When I feel like this, I sometimes would rather avoid talking to you than feel as if my feelings are not being addressed. I would rather address how we both feel about the situation than practicing avoidance."
"You're being an asshole, stop it."	Usually when you ask someone to stop doing something, it's because the action hurts. You could say instead: "I feel hurt when you do/say that. It would be helpful for me if you do not do/say that to me."
"Why do you keep doing that to me?"	"It makes me upset when you keep doing hurtful things to me."
"Sometimes I feel like you're being too inflexible."	Give specific examples; leaving it at this general blanket statement is as unhelpful as saying the original judgmental "you" statement. Also include, "I feel uncomfortable when you don't consider my point of view."

Emotional Support

Jacks McNamara

On-the-Ground Support

M any Occupy sites are establishing a variety of support teams to address the emotional needs of protesters; we deeply respect their (our, your) ongoing openness, compassion, and commitment to dialogue, people, and the Occupy movement. This section offers tips for approaching distress and disturbance on the ground at Occupy through a radical mental health lens.

Ongoing Spaces and Trainings

Create a Support area that is separate from, although possibly nearby, a Medical area and offers a space for people to process distress and madness in a way that is safe, calm, politicized, and creative. It could be staffed with volunteer peer supporters, massage therapists, counselors, acupuncturists, mediators, listeners, and/or social workers. It could be stocked with art supplies, books, stories, and other materials that help people explore what is going on for them through a range of means and from a range of different perspectives. The more diverse the better!

Form a group whose purpose is to support the emotional well-being of all involved. In some Occupy sites, groups working on this have called themselves "Support," "Emotional First Aid," and/or "Safer Spaces." Some of these groups may focus on specific areas within the emotional health framework. These groups may form a Safety Structure connecting with groups such as Security/Community Alliance, Medics, or Empathy/Nonviolent Communication groups to develop creative ideas and collaborate on a sustainable encampment/protest. Emotional support folks might consider wearing an easily identifiable item such as certain color armbands.

Together these groups may create protocols for dealing with crises that the various Working Groups involved agree to follow. For instance, when faced with people yelling at one another, rather than immediately calling for Security, some Occupy sites call first for Support. The emotional support people try to de-escalate and assess the situation. If needed, then Security may be called for. Try to keep your focus on support and inclusion, as opposed to security and exclusion.

Host teach-ins with the on-site protesters that both reduce fear and "Othering" around distress and madness and promote emotional well-being as holistic, collective, political, and in many ways created by the community through the development of an atmosphere that supports expression, connection, and nourishment. Encourage people to set up peer-support groups around social and emotional well-being.

Recognize that you/we are protesters, too! Many activists quit being active because they become exhausted, burned out, and/or traumatized. It follows that we need to both witness personal experiences of suffering—and honor the long-term sustainability of protest and revolution—by taking care of ourselves and each other. When it comes to emotional support, we must all practice what we preach; process is the product. If things gets rough for you, if you're feeling upset or triggered, never hesitate to step out and/or talk with someone. Do shifts in pairs or small groups, hold regular meetings to think/talk through or role-play challenging situations, and designate specific times for debrief and recreation.

Psychological First Aid

Psychological first aid documents ideas for responding to urgent situations in which someone is experiencing marked distress or madness, whether a panic attack during a march, trauma following police brutality, or an aggressive on-site disturbance late at night. Above all, the people who engage in psychological first aid must not be afraid of emotional intensity. They need to be able to enter it with the person, while remaining one hundred percent present and conscious of their interaction and surroundings.

Safety: Build the person's sense of safety and control by removing them from harm's way and possibly the scene. Embody a sense of community, compassion, inclusion, security, and shelter: Ask, "What do you need right now?" or "How can I help you in this moment?" Right off the bat, meet their basic needs (food, water, ice, tea, a phone call, and/or medical attention). You might try giving simple either/or choices ("Would you like a piece of fruit or a Luna bar?" or "Can I get you a cup of tea or some ice water?") This gives people something to focus on and a sense of control in the simplest form, without overwhelming them with too many choices. Be clear and concise with your communication, and reduce any other stressors, including bystanders and extraneous support people.

Comfort: Practice stress reduction/management through techniques such as breathing and body awareness. Ask them what's up/what happened, but be cautious of re-traumatization: let them lead the conversation. Provide soothing human contact (first asking consent to physically touch the person); comfort and console. Validate their experiences as common and expected, without minimizing what they are going through. Remember that feelings are always subjective, and therefore always 100 percent real.

Language: Be aware of, and sensitive to, your language. Consider that many occupiers may find clinical language to be triggering and oppressive. Remember that people come from diverse backgrounds and perspectives, and language is often used as a tool to marginalize and control, and our movement is still developing a compassionate language for describing altered states of mind that respects people's subjective experiences. Try to be humble when judging another person's state of mind. Stick to concrete descriptions and the words the person uses, and be aware that some things that may seem helpful can actually be harmful. For example, do not say, "Lets talk about something else," "You should try to get over this," "You're strong enough to deal with this," "I know how you feel," "You'll feel better soon," "You need to relax," "It's good that you are alive," "It's a good thing you didn't get arrested," or "It's a good thing you got out of there before they whipped out the rubber bullets." These comments could pathologize and exacerbate the traumatic experiences of the person you are trying to support.

Connectedness: A sense of isolation can be extremely distressing in and of itself. Keep or get people connected to their friends, communities, loved ones, and the broader Occupy movement. With their permission, you may need to make contact with people on their behalf. Provide pathways for them to gain social support from others who are coping with the same traumatic experience. Offer material about the different resources and services available both within and beyond Occupy, taking care to explain that their experiences are unique, contextual, transitional, and can be engaged with a diverse range of approaches.

Self-determination: Talk with people about their situation. Using your best judgment, give them information that they want about what happened/is happening/will happen. Clarify things only to the extent that you are absolutely sure; do not set people up for unreasonable expectations. For example, it is better to say "I don't know, but I can try to help you find out where your friends are" rather than "I've heard that the National Lawyers Guild lawyers are getting everyone out tonight!" Start turning their care back over to them. Develop a plan of immediate first steps for what to do when they leave, using practical first steps and do-able tasks, before brainstorming with them about how they might start to plan for longer-term support if needed.

Active listening: We all have two ears and one mouth; we should be listening twice as much as we speak. Remember that people often just need and want to be heard more than anything else. Make it clear that you are listening:

♥ Body language: leaning in, eye contact, facial expressions, minimal fidgeting

♥ A compassionate presence: calm, soothing tone of voice; minimal encouragement (saying yes/ nodding/ summarizing/ mirroring/ reflecting); let them drive the conversation—start with a clear and open mind, and do not come to the conversation with expectations; occasionally repeat what you are hearing in your own words; ask questions to clarify if necessary; do not interrupt; be very careful with humor (no sarcasm)

♥ Active understanding: avoid asking "Why?" and "Why not?"; do not judge; silence is okay, but be sure to continue eye contact or (again, consensual) touch

Suicidal Thoughts, Violence, and Hospitalization

If someone seems suicidal, speak with them. Listen to their feelings before telling them to do anything. Ask directly if they are considering killing themselves. Ask if they have a tool or a plan. If so, ask if they can trust you enough to share the plan or give you the tools they were going to use. Also, ask if they have executed the plan already (for example, if they've taken pills). It is also beneficial to ask something like, "Have you felt this way before? If so, how did you overcome this feeling?" This enables you to see how the person was able to feel better in previous episodes. Most of all, take it very seriously. Read about suicide risks and signs. Call the local suicide crisis hotline, and talk over the situation with them.

Hospitals are not a panacea and can sometimes make things worse. While it is harder to kill yourself in a hospital than outside, it still happens. Someone who is kicked out of the hospital due to insurance or other policies may then kill themselves in the end. If the suicidal person is hospitalized, have a support team visit during and after hospitalization. Ideally, the person being hospitalized makes the decision to go; in many states, it is not possible to admit someone without their consent.

Don't take the decision to hospitalize someone lightly. How bad can a few days or weeks or months in a psych ward be? Worse than jail? For some, yes. Inpatient hospitalization often inflicts physical and emotional abuse on patients, with scars and medical bills that can last a lifetime. Once hospitalized, many patients are sucked into a revolving door of psychiatric care as their personalities are dissected and pathologized under the gaze of the psychiatric magnifying glass. If possible, provide an alternative space to a hospital. Some have found that time at a spa or even a hotel room, with friends present around the clock, is far more effective than a hospital stay. Perhaps the suicidal person would like a healing ceremony of sorts.

It is impossible to judge the level of risk of suicide. If nothing else, do not keep it to yourself. Speak with crisis workers. Keep a close eye on the person. Encourage them to come talk to you and other emotional support people as often as they want. Be especially worried if, after earlier confiding their suicidality, they seem to suddenly withdraw or act especially happy. They may have made a decision to kill themselves, which may be giving them a sense of peace.

Don't diagnose violent behavior. When support gets called in, it's often because someone is being disruptive or harmful to others. This could be anything from loud, off-topic rants at a meeting to physical or sexual violence. When someone is acting in harmful ways and the cause isn't immediately apparent, it can be tempting to try to "diagnose" them and to conflate actions taken to prevent them from harming others with actions taken to help them. But confusing the two can be really hurtful, both to the person you're trying to help (a lot of the trauma around psychiatric abuse stems from coercive and hurtful acts performed in the name of helping the person) and to people in mental distress who are not harming others but may get lumped in with those who are. Remember that fear and anxiety may heighten the tension, so try to remain calm and avoid accusations and blame.

An alternative approach for dealing with violent disruptions is to first concentrate on meeting the needs of the community by leading the disruptive person out of the common space. Talk to them patiently and ask them what's going on while escorting them to a calmer setting. If that doesn't work, you may have to physically separate the person from the altercation, but verbal de-escalation should always be the first and second choice. Once the person is in a space, physically and/or emotionally, where they are not likely to harm others, only then can you focus on their needs. Ask them what they need, and see what you can do to help them get more local resources or connect with their support network. Whatever action is taken to help them should be with the person's full consent.

If someone is physically attacking people, groping people, or stealing stuff, the community may decide to take further action to protect itself. These situations are extraordinarily complex, and there is no formula that applies in all contexts. Unfortunately, we do not all share a compassionate language for thinking and talking about these issues. Wherever possible, try to involve the offender's friends and allies when formulating a response, and listen to the voices and stories of ex-prisoners and psychiatric survivors when considering difficult actions.

If there is a weapon involved, try to convince the person to give it to you. If they will not, and if trying all your de-escalation or intervention tactics, and those of others in the group, does not work, it may be necessary to call for police assistance for the greater well-being of all. Perhaps that person can return another time, but at the moment, they are not acting in a way that is conducive to everyone else's health nor their own.

If considering hospitalization or incarceration, take responsibility for your decisions and be clear about your motives—it'll make your presence more effective. Don't send someone to the hospital or call the police because it's "better than doing nothing." Let people know about community resources, and together figure out ways to meet their needs without harming others. Calling the police or sending someone to the emergency room for mental health concerns should be a last resort, after consultation with friends and allies. Consider first the potential ramifications including imprisonment, deportation/loss of immigration status, increased depression, undue medication, shame, a prison record, loss of custody/visitation rights, interruption of life, loss of anonymity, and health care debt, as well as further scrutiny of protests, police brutality, sensationalist media representations, and so on.

If someone is hospitalized or incarcerated, follow through by organizing visits and other communication. When they come out, help them process why the support team made the decisions they did. Try to be receptive to their critique and/or anger and/or gratitude.

Try to see every action taken by those within the movement, whether positive or negative, welcome or unwelcome, as an opportunity to come together as a community and support one another. Choosing to alienate others or ourselves in times of stress creates a snowball effect of hurt feelings and hurtful actions. However alone we may sometimes feel, we are all in this together.

Navigating Crisis

Bexa

When It All Comes Crashing Down

When you or someone close to you goes into crisis, it can be the scariest thing to ever happen. You don't know what to do, but it seems like someone's life might be at stake or they might get locked up, and everyone around is getting stressed and panicked. Most people have either been there themselves or know a friend who has been there. Someone's personality starts to make strange changes, they're not sleeping or sleeping all day, they lose touch with the people around them, they disappear into their room for days, they have wild energy and outlandish plans, they start to dwell on suicide and hopelessness, they stop eating or taking care of themselves, or they start taking risks, being reckless, and may (in rare circumstances) become frustrated and violent towards themselves or others. They become a different person. They're in crisis.

The word "crisis" comes from the greek word *krisis* meaning "decision" or "judgment." A crisis is a moment of great tension and meeting the unknown. It's a turning point when things can't go on the way they have, and the situation isn't going to hold. Could crisis be an opportunity for breakthrough, not just breakdown? Can we learn about each other and ourselves as a community through crisis? Can we see crisis as an opportunity to judge a situation and ourselves carefully, not just react with panic and confusion or turn things over to the authorities? While everyone must be held accountable for their words and behavior, it is our collective responsibility to create a space for this to occur in a way that promotes movement, not containment, in people's lives.

Crisis Response Suggestions

Work together.

If you're trying to help someone in crisis, coordinate with others to share responsibility and stress. If you're the one going through crisis, you may want to reach out to multiple people whom you trust. Human connection can be very healing for a crisis. The more people you have to support you, the easier the process will be and the less you will exhaust your support system.

Try not to panic.

Crisis can be made a lot worse if people start reacting with fear, control, and anger. Study after study has shown that if you react to someone in crisis with caring, openness, patience, and a relaxed and unhurried attitude, it can really help settle things down. Often times this approach is derailed because the supporters themselves are exhausted and stressed. Above all, the people who engage in crisis support must not be afraid of emotional intensity and altered states—they need to be able to both enter it with the person, and remain one hundred percent present and conscious of their interaction and surroundings.

Be real about what's going on.

When people act weird or lose their minds, it is easy to overreact. It's also easy to underreact. If someone picks up a knife and is walking around talking about UFOs, don't assume the worst and call the cops. If someone is actually seriously attempting suicide or doing something extremely dangerous like lying down on a busy freeway, getting the police involved might save their life, but it might also put them through more trauma from being forcibly locked up in a hospital ward. Likewise, if someone is cutting themselves, it doesn't always mean they're suicidal. People cut for a variety of reasons, most of which are deeply personal and incapable of being understood through diagnosis. Sometimes people who are talking about the ideas of death and suicide are in a very dangerous place, but sometimes they may just need to talk about dark, painful feelings that are buried. Use your judgment, and don't be afraid to ask others for advice. Also, don't be afraid to ask the person in crisis what they need. Sometimes you just need to wait out crisis. Sometimes you do need to make the difficult decision to take action to try to interrupt a pattern or cycle. What that action is can depend on a lot of things, like the person's trauma history, their physical needs, and the availability of support networks.

Listen to the person without judgment.

What do they need? What are their feelings? What's going on? What can help? Sometimes we are so scared of someone else's suffering that we forget to ask them how we can help. Beware of arguing with someone in crisis: their point of view might be off, but their feelings are real and need to be listened to. (Once they're out of crisis, they'll be able to hear you better.) If you are in crisis, tell people what you're feeling and what you need. It is so hard to help people who aren't communicating.

Lack of sleep is a major contributor to crisis.

Many people come right out of crisis if they get some sleep, and any hospital will first try to get them to sleep if they are sleep deprived. Sometimes the psychiatric drugs hospitals provide can really help with sleep, but sometimes the lack of privacy and control in the hospital environment can itself cause or worsen insomnia. If the person hasn't tried Benadryl, herbal or homeopathic remedies from a health food store, hot baths, rich food, exercise, soothing sound, or acupuncture, these can be extremely helpful. If someone is really manic and hasn't been sleeping for months, though, none of these may work and you may have to temporarily seek out psychiatric drugs to break the cycle.

Drugs may also be a big factor in crisis.

Did someone who regularly takes medication suddenly stop? This can cause a crisis because of the severe withdrawal effects of psychiatric drugs, which often get (mis)diagnosed as people's "mental illness" coming back. Ideally, someone quitting medication has a plan and support system in place to do so, but in the absence of such, try to respect their wish to go through withdrawal. The crisis may be physically necessary and may pass, although remember that a transition to no psychiatric drugs must be done carefully and slowly, not suddenly. If they are not deliberately trying to come off of their drugs, try to help them to get back on them.

Create a sanctuary, and meet basic needs.

Try to de-dramatize and de-stress the situation as much as possible. Crashing in a different space for a few days can give a person some breathing space and perspective. Perhaps caring friends could come by in shifts to spend time with the person, make good food, play nice music, drag them outside for fresh air and movement, and spend time listening. Often people feel alone and uncared for in crisis, and if you make an effort to offer them a sanctuary it can mean a lot. Make sure basic needs are met: food, water, sleep, shelter, exercise, friendship, and if appropriate, professional (alternative or psychiatric) attention.

Calling the police or hospital shouldn't be the automatic response.

Police and hospitals are not saviors. They can even make things worse. When you're out of other options, though, you shouldn't rule them out. Faced with a decision like this, try and get input from people who are thinking clearly and know about the person. Have other options been tried? Did the hospital help in the past? Were police and hospitals traumatizing? Are people overreacting? Don't assume that it's always the right thing to do just because it puts everything in the hands of the "authorities." Be realistic, however, when your community has exhausted its capacity to help and there is a risk of real danger. The alternative support networks we need do not exist everywhere people are in crisis. If someone does get hospital or doctor care, be cautious about any diagnosis they receive. Sometimes labels can be helpful, but madness is ultimately mysterious and diagnoses aren't scientific or objective. Labels can confine us to a narrow medical perspective of our experience and needs and limit our sense of possibility. Having a disease label is not the only way to take someone's pain seriously and get help. If someone is hospitalized, try to visit them, or call if you can't visit. Knowing someone on the outside cares for them can mean a lot.

First Aid for Emotional Trauma

Trauma (or post-traumatic stress) is the emotional "shock" after a life-threatening, violent event. Anything that makes our body panic and go into a fight/ flight/freeze response can leave us traumatized. The effects may be immediate or take time to surface, and can be felt for the rest of our lives.

Being traumatized is a **normal response to an extreme situation;** even "tough" people like mothers or seasoned political activists can be traumatized. Emotional traumatization happens to everyone, no matter how "hardcore" they are. There is a tendency in activist circles for some folks to act heroic in the face of trauma. It is perfectly common, even expected, to respond to experiences of police violence and rough protest street scenes in extreme ways.

The causes of trauma can include almost anything: disaster, abuse, rape, witnessing violence, loss, or spending time with people who are traumatized. Because **trauma happens when our bodies perceive our lives are in danger and we can't escape**, medical surgeries, emotional abuse, or loss of a loved one or home can also be traumatic. Even though two people may experience a similar event, one may feel traumatized by it, while the other does not. It is important not to judge others for their experience of trauma.

Trauma means getting **stuck in the memory** of a life- threatening event. Our bodies and minds act like the event is still happening, right now, even though it is in the past.

We are on guard, defensive, and "geared up," or hopeless, paralyzed, and numb. We avoid things that remind us of the past and trigger painful memories, and we isolate ourselves from others and limit our freedom. We block out unpleasant memories and feelings, sometimes turning to drugs and alcohol. We repeat past situations. We have panic attacks or go into jumpy "fight-flight" mode, even when there is no real danger in the present. Our lives, health, and relationships with other people suffer, and **we live constrained and limited by our past**. Sometimes we take our pain out on others, or become self-destructive.

Emotional Support

In the past these trauma responses were crucial to our survival, and in the present they protect us from being overwhelmed. When we value the usefulness of our trauma coping mechanisms, forgiveness and acceptance can invite gradual change.

Unfortunately **trauma is usually not a wound that heals just by waiting** for time to pass. Trauma can keep hold of our lives for many years. It is important to try to work with the trauma somehow, in whatever way is best for you.

Making connections with others and honestly expressing our feelings is important, especially when we want to hide or avoid our problems. **Finding safety and trust is the first step to healing.**

Just talking, though, may not be enough to heal trauma. **Sometimes talking about what happened can mean *reliving* what happened**, and not help. If the talking seems to go in circles or not lead to a sense of completion, it might be just stirring things up, not healing them.

It is also commonly believed that you can heal trauma by "getting it out of your system," punching pillows, or venting strong emotions. This can be helpful, but sometimes it can end up making things worse, or even re-traumatize you. **Real trauma healing is usually slower and more gentle.**

Therapy, including EMDR, DBT, and CBT, can help many people. Others find these are not helpful. This section focuses on what we can do for each other as a community. Most importantly, **everyone is an individual—experiment and discover what works for you** and learn how to best help yourself and others.

Signs of a traumatized or "triggered" state:

- Repetitive thinking of worrying thoughts or memories related to the event; intrusive memories and feelings; chronic fear

- Staring off into space; "thousand yard stare;" flattened or frozen expression and body; freezing and numbing; "emptiness"

- Extreme defensiveness and rigid thinking; irritability; explosive overreactions

- Sexual preoccupation and constant interest

- Discomfort, pain, stress, illness; "nervios"

- Returning to traumatizing situations

When someone has just been traumatized:

1. Help any bodily injury, medical issue, or physical need first

2. Don't get up and act like nothing happened

3. Go to a safe place; help them to stay dry, warm, and still

4. If the person wants to talk, listen without interrupting or changing the subject

5. Remember that trembling or being emotional is part of healing, and better than "numbing out;" encourage people to feel the sensations in their body fully. (See below.)

First Aid/Feeling Body Sensations:

Trauma cuts us off from our bodies. When we are in overwhelming danger, we dissociate or "leave our bodies" as a protective measure. Later this protective mechanism becomes stuck and counterproductive. The **key to healing trauma is to return to our bodies**, by feeling our physical sensations and making our bodies safe and alive again.

Ask, "How do you know that you are sad? Is there tightness in your chest or throat? How do you know you are afraid? Is there a cold feeling, or a sinking feeling in your stomach? Feel it fully. How large is the feeling? Is it changing? What do you feel next?" Listen without interruption and give plenty of time to feel and respond. Grounding and resourcing yourself will also help the other person.

Keeping eyes open usually is best for focusing on body sensations.

If the person can't feel their body at all, ask, "Can you feel your feet on the ground? Your pelvis sitting on the chair?" Grasp their hand or shoulder and say "Can you feel my hand?" **Always ask before touching.** If lying down, ask them to sit up. Ask to walk around slowly and feel their legs and feet. Or gently hold and press their feet to the ground.

If the person is staring off in the distance, talking in circles, withdrawn, or agitated, encourage them to put their attention to the world. Ask, "Look around—what colors do you see? Can you name them?" Ask them what sensations they feel in their bodies.

When someone is preoccupied with traumatic memories, find distractions. Ask them, "When was a time that you felt safe and peaceful? Can you describe the sights, sounds, smells and colors of that time?" Ask them to feel sensations in their body.

If the person is defensive, on guard and uncooperative, just drop it. Change the subject, go for a walk, leave the discussion/work for later. When a traumatized and defensive person perceives you as a threat, it is very difficult to convince them to just "snap out of it" or to see that they are experiencing a flashback. Wait until they are calm to discuss it.

If body sensations are too uncomfortable, try to find a sensation, even small, that is neutral or pleasant, and focus on it. Go back and forth between uncomfortable and pleasant senations. Notice any relaxation in breathing, warmth, or trembling. This is normal; feel the sensations fully.

Feelings of fear, guilt, loss, sadness, or anger are normal when we are traumatized. Don't judge feelings in yourself or others. Listen with acceptance and care.

Ongoing Support

Triggers: It can be helpful to make a list of situations and things that trigger traumatic memories and upset you. Anniversaries of events, people, places, and situations can all be triggers. Learn to avoid your triggers, expose yourself gradually, or prepare for them when they come. Ask friends to help you.

Resourcing: Write down a list of things that make your body feel strong and safe. It can be anything, such as walking or taking baths, exercising or sports, listening to music or petting your dog. Add things you've done in the past and would like to do again. Keep the list and add to it with new resources you find.

Breathing: Relaxed, deep breathing can often bring relief from trauma symptoms. Sit comfortably and gently fill your belly, chest, and shoulders on the in breath, and exhale your shoulders, chest, and belly. Breath comfortably—don't push or use effort—but allow yourself to take slow, deep breaths. A few minutes of breathing this way can help calm you down.

Physical health: Trauma survivors have weakened immune systems and are more vulnerable to getting sick. Get adequate rest and fresh water, go to nature, exercise, and avoid junk food. Consider a good-quality multi-vitamin/multi-mineral supplement, with plenty of C and B.

Psychiatric drugs: Anti-depressants, tranquilizers (benzodiazepines), and other psychiatric drugs may provide short term relief and can help with extreme anxiety and sleeplessness. However, these drugs have very risky side effects and are toxic to the body. Long-term use can lead to addiction, make sleeplessness and anxiety worse, interfere with the natural healing process, and overdose can be fatal. Avoid or use cautiously.

Alternative medicines: Herbs, traditional remedies, and holistic care can be very effective for trauma. For example, after 9-11 and Hurricane Katrina, acupuncturists gave immediate relief to trauma survivors, including firefighters and medical personnel.

Written by Will Hall: wiltonhall@gmail.com. (with edits by Occupy Mental Health group, 2011) Sources: Peter Levine, Judith Herman. Thanks: Julie Diamond. 12-08 version.

Bexa

A lmost all movements for change have had to deal with issues of power, privilege, patriarchy, internal racism, etc. Though these are the things we are working to change in our larger world (domination, oppression, greed, etc.), we've all grown up in these worlds of inequality, so it's unfortunate, but we often end up a microcosm with similar problems. Tragically, sexual assault is one of these rampant problems, and some people have sexually assaulted people within some Occupy encampments. Different Occupy groups will grapple with these issues in diverse ways, but here's some ideas. We've seen amazing work done by people in Occupy groups on this rotten reality—working to create an environment where these violations are less likely to occur, and to provide support if they do! A strong movement works to address its own issues, while connecting them with the larger issues they are addressing. There are many resources and models to draw from out there for dealing with these issues. See the appendix for more.

Basic Steps to Preventing Sexual Assault

While nothing can prevent people from doing awful things, there are certain policies that Occupy groups could adopt that might help:

♥ Ask consent before touching. That means ask, "Can I hug you? Kiss you?" etc, and wait for the person to reply yes or no, instead of just going ahead and touching a person.

♥ Develop a system for dealing with assaults/boundary breaches to hold people accountable for their actions, and support all involved. Unaddressed problems within movements destroy them.

♥ Provide teach-ins on abuse cycles, consent, and sexual assault.

♥ Make it a priority that no one is forced to sleep near people they don't know.

♥ Make safer sleeping areas. Some Occupy Wall Street groups have created areas for women-identified people and people with kids, as well as sober and queer- and/or trans-friendly areas.

Emotional Support

♥ Create an overall space that values gender and sexual diversity; these values should be actively woven through all aspects of the Occupy sites, processes, and actions.

Occupy Wall Street Safer Spaces Training Document

Principles for anti-oppression

♥ Practice listening.

♥ Be aware of your own privilege and the space you occupy.

♥ Understand that your experience is your own; don't normalize it to the exclusion of others.

♥ Validate other people's experiences of racism, sexism, homophobia, transphobia, ableism and other forms of oppression and work to counter them.

♥ Don't make assumptions about people's identities.

♥ Do not engage in silencing behavior; make room for everyone to speak.

Principles for survivor support

♥ Believe the person when they tell you they were harmed.

♥ Give agency to the person harmed to make their own decisions.

♥ Enforce separation from the perpetuator if requested in order to provide safety.

♥ Don't assume what the person harmed needs: ask and offer options.

- Ask before engaging in any physical contact, even if it seems harmless.

- Try to keep the person engaged and present.

- Recognize triggers and try to limit them.

De-escalation and nonviolent communication tactics

- Speak from "I."

- Practice listening.

- Take a walk if needed to remove the person from the space.

- Identify and name problematic behaviors.

- Acknowledge your own and the other person's emotions (e.g. "It seems like we're both tired.")

- Mirror the other person's nonviolent actions and mannerisms to make them comfortable.

- Be compassionate but be honest.

How to respond to an incident

- End the immediate harm.

- De-escalate and separate.

- Ask the person who was harmed about their needs and allow the person to make choices.

- Follow up.

Healing from Sexual Assault

Individuals

Healing from sexual assault is similar to other types of traumas but unique in its own ways, too. If friends, family, and one's community respond with care and support that further empowers the survivor, it can help in the survivor's recovery process.

Sexual assault survivors are often left with extreme feelings of shame, humiliation, powerlessness, and fear. The person who was assaulted (survivor) must be in charge of their followup. They need to know that they alone get to decide whether to go to a hospital for a forensic medical exam (commonly known as a "rape kit"), or notify police. A support person can offer suggestions but can't force the survivor to do anything.

A supporter should offer to accompany the survivor to a hospital or in dealing with a police report but should not pressure them to do either. The supporter should not touch the survivor unless given consent. If the survivor does not want to file a police report, ask them what they want to happen to the perpetrator. Let the survivor know that they do not need to make these decisions right away. However, if there is any chance that the person might consider a medical exam and/or legal proceedings, it is best if they do not shower or bathe right away because evidence will be lost. Overall, the supporter must assure the survivor that they will do all they can to support them and that the community will stand by the survivor's wishes. The supporter must also do what they can to assure the survivor's anonymity within the community.

It may be helpful to speak anonymously with a counselor at a rape crisis center directly by calling the National Sexual Assault Hotline at 1.800.656.HOPE. It will connect you with a local rape crisis center.

Many resources are listed at **www.rainn.org/get-information**.

Community

Groups may want to provide further counseling for people who are in any way affected by a sexual assault, or by how the community has dealt with it. They may also want to provide conflict resolution/mediation as a format for people to talk things through.

Some Occupy sites have groups which specifically formed to provide support and visibility for survivor issues and issues of consent. They have created wonderful documents for accountability processes, for supporting survivors, and for community response protocols. They have worked to educate everyone engaging with Occupy about sexual assault, domestic violence, and consent. They have created trainings for people who take shifts to be on call at the encampment if an event arises. Some have released press statements in response to sexual assaults that happened at their Occupy site. Safer Spaces in NYC released a statement about a sexual assault which happened at OWS: www.nycga.net/groups/safer-spaces-committee/docs/transforming-harm-building-safety-confronting-sexual-violence-at-occupy-wall-street-beyond-2

Peer Support and Mutual Aid

By the Icarus Project

Jacks McNamara

Mutual Aid Groups and Listening Spaces

Breaking through the walls and making a connection can mean all the difference in the world.

Mutual aid and support groups are a way to bring down the walls that isolate us. No one in the group is above anyone else: mutual aid means we listen to and support each other as a community of equals, without paid professionals or staff to define who we are. Each of us is an expert on our own experience, and each of us is the center for our decisions— and we are not alone.

When we gather together with people who've been through what we've been through, people who share some of the mysteries and suffering that get labeled "mental illness," we discover new maps through crisis, learn new tools to stay healthy, and weave communities of solidarity to change the world. We discover something at the heart of the dangerous gift of madness: caring for others is often the best way to care for ourselves.

Listening Spaces

There is a wide diversity of group models to draw on, and we encourage you to experiment to find the best fit for you. All these approaches, however, share the same essential principle: create a space for listening.

In nature, stillness, silence, and sky create a vast container for what is essential to emerge. Step into wilderness and you encounter a hushed patience and gentle holding rare in the noisy, sped-up clash and clamor of our lives. Corporate monocropped culture suppresses true listening and imposes labels, rigid habits, and preconceived notions. Real support and caring means breaking down habitual ways of interacting, and meeting each other in spaces of true, effective listening.

Key elements of listening spaces

♥ Don't talk over others or interrupt. If someone interrupts, gently ask them to stop. Take turns. Raise hands, or go in order.

♥ Don't rush through or go too fast. Create a calm, quiet space without interruptions or distractions.

♥ Allow periods of silence while we find what to say.

♥ Let the person decide when they are done. Don't jump in. If time is an issue, the group should decide on what's fair and stick to it.

♥ Don't react or speak up automatically. Watch how your reactions to what others say reflect your own experience, not the person speaking. Give yourself time to respond from a deeper place.

♥ Ask permission before giving advice or responding directly to what someone said. Sometimes people just want to be listened to.

♥ When someone responds to you or gives advice, allow yourself to take what is helpful from options presented, and leave the rest, rather than defending yourself if you disagree.

♥ Listen as a receiver, not as a critic. Imagine different perspectives and experiences, rather than assuming they're just like yours.

Facilitation and Self-Facilitation

With their roots in effective listening, groups can nurture healing and community through facilitation. Facilitators help the group listen more effectively, and pay specific attention to the overall needs and direction of everyone involved, not just their own individual needs. The facilitator should avoid bias, and if they are too involved with a particular group topic then someone else might be better in the role. It helps when two people facilitate and when facilitators reflect group diversity such as gender, age, and race. It is also good to pair more experienced and less experienced facilitators, and to offer new people a chance to learn facilitation skills.

Importantly, everyone should keep overall group needs in mind, and everyone can assist the group through self-facilitation.

Key elements of facilitation and self-facilitation

♥ Create a clear agenda or plan on how to spend your time together.

♥ Keep track of time so people can "wrap up" their feelings without feeling cut off or not heard. Closing the meeting respectfully is as important as beginning it.

♥ Remind everyone to respect group confidentiality, so sensitive information does not leave the room.

♥ Check in with the group's energy level and focus, and redirect the conversation if it is becoming scattered or bogged down. Suggest breaks, exercises, games, or agenda and time revisions when necessary. If conversation is lagging, ask questions, tell a story, or get up and do some stretching. Sometimes if the group is stuck, the facilitator can ask a clarifying question, reframe an issue, or connect points to earlier discussion.

♥ Offer choices, especially if people want feedback or not after they speak.

♥ Consider using "I" statements when speaking, such as "I feel" and "I want," to stay focused on your own feelings and needs. Talking about other people or gossiping takes focus away from your own experience.

♥ Encourage defining problems within the concept of "dangerous gifts" and unique mysterious talents rather than seeing ourselves as flawed or diseased.

♥ Use a common vocabulary and minimize jargon.

♥ Be on the lookout for repeating patterns in each other's lives to identify root causes.

♥ Investigate how past experiences shape present realities. Did something from childhood happen this way? From an early work or school experience? The past can help explain the present, but stay focused on present problems.

♥ Reflect upon the political dimension of personal problems, and reframe problems within a framework of a crazy-making society instead of blaming the person suffering.

♥ Hold people accountable for behaviors but don't criticize who they are as people.

♥ Focus on the things we can control and let go of things we can't, but don't give up on visions of change and revolution!

♥ Keep an experimental attitude and a willingness to explore new perspectives and options.

♥ Learn what triggers you and how to cope with them. Recognize the buildup, escalations and de-escalations in crisis periods.

♥ Remember that the group is not a promise that problems will be solved, but a space to address problems safely.

♥ And finally: know when to bust out! Nature isn't always neat and orderly. Sometimes wild conversation, spontaneity, and "breaking all the rules of facillitation" is exactly what the group needs in the moment. A skilled facilitator and skilled participants can feel when the chaos and cacophany that erupt are refreshing and true to the group spirit, and when to go with it. Then comes the time to reel it all back in and return to the basic structure of taking turns and listening carefully.

Inclusion and Self-Determination

Groups need to be welcoming and inclusive, where diverse perspectives and life choices are respected and honored according to the principles of harm reduction and self-determination. For example, people who take psychiatric drugs and people who don't take them are welcome.

People who use diagnosis categories like "bipolar" to describe themselves, as well as people who define themselves differently, are also welcome.

Ways to create group inclusion

♥ Invite newcomers to introduce themselves if they want to.

♥ Practice "stepping up, stepping back" so we can each contribute to equal participation.

♥ Give priority to people who haven't yet spoken.

Meeting Agreements

This gathering has some basic agreements to ensure inclusion, safety, and open dialogue:

- We "listen like allies." We respect a wide diversity of choices and perspectives, even when we disagree, and we don't judge or invalidate other people's experiences. We try not to interrupt. When it's our turn to speak, we can ask others for feedback and advice, or just have people listen without responding. All responses are in a positive spirit of support and respect.

- We also practice "step up, step back." People who are quiet are encouraged to speak, and those who talk a lot are encouraged to give others a chance. We invite new people to introduce themselves if they want. And silence is also always ok.

- As a community, we try to use "owl vision," the ability to listen closely to the speaker while also having a feeling for the needs of the whole group. Keep in mind that others might be waiting to speak, or when we all might need to take a break.

- We recognize that overcoming oppression helps everyone's liberation; it is the group's responsibility to challenge racism, classism, sexism, ageism, homophobia, and other forms of

♥ Encourage quiet people to speak, but don't require them to or put them on the spot.

♥ Be careful to not dominate the discussion, speak in capital letters, restate what others say, or speak for others.

♥ Allow each person to define their problems the way they want. Don't label or judge others.

♥ If you disagree with someone, ask questions to understand their point of view better. This is not a time for arguments or trying to convince others you're right.

---

prejudice. We educate each other in the spirit of solidarity and hold others accountable for their behavior without criticizing who they are as people.

- We respect spiritual beliefs, altered states of consciousness, and definitions of reality that fall outside the mainstream material view.

- In order to be as clear as possible, we try to use "I" statements when speaking to the group. This helps us avoid misunderstandings, and invokes trust and sensitivity.

- We try to pay attention to repeating patterns in each other's lives, in order to identify root causes. We try to notice common themes and roles that we play out together as a group.

- To create trust we respect confidentiality. The group decides on what level of disclosure and openness outside the group we want.

This is a work in progress. We need everyone's feedback and ideas of how to improve our efforts and strengthen our group. And as we meet, keep in mind that there are many other people gathering like this to build community support networks with a vision of a new world.

♥ Respect different views and choices, such as diagnosis, medication, recreational drugs, nutrition, medical care, holistic health, exercise, spirituality, lifestyle, and other decisions. Change is difficult! People grow at their own pace, and you may not really know what is best for another person, because you are not them.

♥ Accommodate limitations and access needs, such as mobility accessibility and sign language interpretation. Be aware of how choices of where to hold meetings might affect people, such as institutional settings like clinics or health centers that can trigger painful memories, or places with toxic substances (fresh paint, new furniture or carpets) that people might be chemically sensitive to.

♥ Identify and discuss how power and privilege play out by understanding how white supremacy, patriarchy, classism, heterosexism, ableism, and all other forms of oppression affect each of us.

♥ Intervene in situations where people are making oppressive comments. Re-focus on the agenda, and remind everyone of the need for group safety. Recognize the intention behind someone's word choice, and give them an opportunity to correct themselves or recognize how their words might be offensive. It can help to say, "When I just heard you say that, some people might feel you used an inappropriate or disrespectful term. Can you reword that statement?"

♥ Remember that including marginalized voices and overcoming oppression helps everyone's liberation.

When we listen to each other effectively, we begin to understand our needs and how to meet them. Icarus groups can become places to nurture community networks of mutual aid and advocacy, help each other through crisis, deal with the mental health system, and learn about new options and resources.

Mutual Aid

♥ Ensure people can make their own best decisions by having solid facts about the drugs they take, their diagnosis, and options. Psychiatric drugs are toxic and have huge dangers pharmaceutical companies don't talk about, and diagnostic labels are often misleading and disempowering. At the same time, holistic health doesn't work for everyone, and going off drugs can be risky. Share lists of books, websites, and articles that have information correcting mainstream misinformation.

♥ Compare experiences with herbs and holistic health, medications that are helpful, and different treatments.

♥ Share advice and knowledge on how to reduce and go off medication safely if people want to.

♥ Put together a resource list of area low-cost/sliding scale health care practitioners who are open to non-mainstream views of mental health and recovery: use the Icarus Provider Guidelines and listing.

♥ Help people advocate for themselves with their doctors and health care practitioners; accompany them to appointments.

♥ Advocate for people struggling for justice: publicize human rights violations, connect people to patients advocate organizations, visit hospitals, contact area media, write letters to the editor.

♥ Connect each other with legal aid resources, housing, community gardens, free food and other needs.

♥ If a person is disruptive or needs a lot of attention, consider pairing them up with someone one on one, so they can get the focus they need and the rest of the group can continue.

♥ Set aside issues or conflicts taking a lot of group time to deal with outside of the group. Sometimes interpersonal mediation one on one is better than a group trying to solve a problem between two people.

♥ Share info about activism, community events, and recreation so people can meet outside the group.

♥ Learn ways to help people when things start to come crashing down. Consider creating a crisis plan where people name their early warning signs and describe the support they want if they start to go into crisis.

Different Forms of Peer Counseling Groups

With the principle of listening as the foundation, groups can take many forms. Once weekly, once a month? Is it a drop-in group, or are people committed for a series? Is it open to anyone or does the group select its members? Looking at and learning from different group models can give you a broader sense of what is possible and how to structure your group.

♥ 12-Step Programs such as Alcoholics Anonymous. Group members tell their stories drawing on years of shared wisdom, and follow a stages model of recovery through specific personal and spiritual goals. More experienced members coach newer ones through one-on-one sponsorship.Timers divide up speaking time equally.

♥ Council Process ("Talking Stick" model). Members take turns speaking on a theme or topic without interrupting or responding.

♥ Co-Counseling Dyads: People take turns with equal time in pairs, where one person is the speaker and the other just listens, then they switch.

♥ Skill-share, Resource Sharing, Such as Medicine-Specific, Holistic-Specific, or Advocate-Specific.

♥ Reading / discussion group.The group chooses an article or book to discuss each meeting.

♥ Emotional Support Groups: participants gather because they share a particular problem/theme, such as chronic pain, being a veteran, or suffering grief and loss.

♥ Hearing Voices groups: Small gatherings across England and Europe where people discuss the experience of hearing voices and share ways to cope in a non-judgmental atmosphere.

Empower yourselves to explore different options and create your group the way that works best for everyone

Confidentiality

Revealing intimate information makes people vulnerable. Groups build trust when this vulnerability is respected and cared for. Your group should agree to a confidentiality policy and make sure to practice it.

Some options are

General Experience Only: Members may discuss what they and others say and do with people outside the group, but only generally, without any names, details, or clues about the specific people or events. This is a common policy, used in the NYC Icarus Group and Freedom Center: it supports discussion of sensitive topics such as abuse, criminal behavior, and suicide, while allowing participants to take what they learn to the rest of the world.

Personal Experience Only: "What's said here stays here." Participants may discuss what they themselves say and do with people outside the group, but may not talk about, or even refer generally, to what others say or do. This is a more restrictive policy used for groups, such as 12-step groups, that focus specifically on difficult topics such as addiction and abuse.

Full Disclosure: Group participants are free to talk about anything that happened in the group. While common for activist organizations and public events that want to get the word out freely, this approach should be weighed carefully for groups providing mutual emotional support.

Total Non-Disclosure: Anything said or done is not repeated, or even alluded to generally, to anyone outside the group. This can be useful for a closed group focused on a very sensitive topic, where participants want to go very deeply into personal issues over time. This is a common policy used in the RVA Icarus Group.

Every group has different needs, so while General Experience Only is the most common support group policy, the group should set its own policy. Make sure to explain the confidentiality policy at the beginning of meetings, perhaps as part of the preamble.

Example Peer Support Facilitator Notes

Keep in mind that each group is different and unique and that it may be necessary to review and revise the format of your peer support group and the level of disclosure that is practiced. These are the notes that the facilitators of peer support groups in Richmond, Virginia's Icarus Project group use during weekly peer support groups. Feel free to reuse and remix these notes, or make up your own entirely!

1. Start on time!

2. Choose a facilitator via consensus decision-making.

If someone is uncomfortable with the person offering to facilitate, that person needs to voice their position and put in a downvote. We will only know your comfort level if you tell us!

3. Introductions: Facilitator explains the role of a facilitator.

A facilitator guides the group process so that it flows smoothly. In this way, the facilitator leads the group efficiently, but does not take leadership responsibility. The facilitator makes sure that everyone has an equal amount of time to speak and that no person is speaking over or interrupting someone else. The facilitator also keeps time.

As our group is non-hierarchical, we like to rotate the position of facilitator for each meeting. If you wish to volunteer to facilitate in the future, please raise your hand now or speak with me after the meeting. Inexperienced facilitators may be able to team up with more experienced facilitators. Please do not hesitate to ask questions if you are unsure of what a facilitator does.

4. Introductions: Facilitator introduces the purpose of the group.

You can read the mission statement if you choose (have a flier with the mission statement available)

5. Introductions: Go around the circle with introductions.

Each person introduces themselves. We suggest giving your name and a story of how your personal experience has led you to be interested in radical or alternative mental health in general, or the Icarus Project specifically.

6. Facilitator explains listening spaces/safe spaces.

Icarus Gathering Pre(r)amble

As a group of people inspired by the Icarus Project, we offer you this preamble as a tool for your gatherings. You can summarize or read the preamble out loud to begin your meeting, as a way to focus the purpose and keep the bigger vision in everyone's mind. As your group learns its own lessons and needs, feel free to revise and create your own version.

Welcome everyone to our Icarus Project local gathering!

The Icarus Project envisions a new culture and language that resonates with our actual experiences of 'mental illness' rather than trying to fit our lives into a conventional framework. We see our madness as a dangerous gift to be cultivated and taken care of, rather than as a disease or disorder needing to be "cured" or "overcome."

This is a space for people to come together and learn from each others' different views and experiences of madness. People who take psychiatric drugs are welcome here, as are people who don't take psychiatric drugs. People who use diagnosis categories to describe themselves are welcome, as are people who define themselves differently. The Icarus Project values self-determination and mutual support.

---

7.   Facilitator explains the level of confidentiality that we consented to at the first meeting.

We use general experience only: while in peer support, members may discuss what they and others say and do with people outside the group, but only generally, without using any names, details, or clues about the specific people or events. This supports discussion of sensitive topics such as abuse, criminal behavior, and suicide. This is helpful because many of us may frequent the same places or have the same friends. Someone said at the first meeting that "we do not have consent to use someone's name that is not present."

We also use total non-disclosure. Anything said or done in the group is not repeated, or even alluded to generally, to anyone outside the group. What goes on here stays here.

8.   Individuals start sharing without interruption (<10 people present). Split into smaller groups and start sharing (>10 people present).

If the person has been to peer support in the past, we suggest that they share how they have been feeling since the last time they came. If the person is new to peer support, we suggest that they share how they've been doing recently (i.e. the past few weeks/a month). The person sharing can voice whether they would like a response or if they just want people to listen, and would not like a response at this time.

9.   Responses and feedback for individuals who welcome it.

10. Closing comments/wrapping up.

Encourage members to sign up for email list and to be a crisis line facilitator.

11. Announce the next peer support date!

Emotional Support

Credits, Contributors, and Co-Conspirators

This zine was lovingly created by a community of authors, editors, designers, artists and other contributors. Some of this material was remixed from existing sources, while other works were created especially for this booklet. To contact us, please write to **info@mindfuloccupation.org**.

Cover Design: Tatiana Makovkin

Layout: Cal Moen and HB Lozito

Collaborative Authoring: Aki Imai, Becca Shaw Glaser, Eric Stiens, Jonah Bossewitch, M. Osborn of Mindful Liberation Project (mindfulliberationproject@gmail.com, mindfulliberation.wordpress.com), Rachel Liebert, Sarah Harper (rockharp@gmail.com, www.myspace.com/rockharper), Sascha Altman DuBrul

Editing: Aki Imai, Becca Shaw Glaser, M. Osborn, Rachel Liebert, Cal Moen

Curation (gathering and remixing materials): Aki Imai, Becca Shaw Glaser, Danielle Demos, Eric Stiens, Eric W, irene greene, Jacks McNamara, Jonah Bossewitch, Kim Christoffel, Maryse Mitchell-Brody, M. Osborn, Rachel Liebert, Sadie Robins, sandra@sandrajoneshealing.com, Sascha Altman DuBrul, Tatiana Makovkin

Artwork: Jacks McNamara, Becca Shaw Glaser (bexa.org), Tatiana Makovkin, M. Osborn (mosborn.org), Ira Birch, Fly, Sophie Crumb, Erik Ruin

Catalyst: Jonah Bossewitch

Supporters: { wholespace.collective }, Anita Altman, Barbara Ford, Voices of the Heart Inc., Darby Penney, David Lukoff, Dean Spade, Eve Lindi, Iona Woolmington, Jack Z. Bratich, thecounterbalanceproject. wordpress.com, Beja Alisheva, Shir Yaakov, Travis Mushett, Ken Paul Rosenthal, and a bunch of other great people—thank you so much for supporting our printing and mailing costs!

Notes and Attributions:

"Coping Skills in Times of Stress" was adapted from M. Osborn's *Coping Skills* zine, written for The Icarus Project.

"First Aid for Emotional Trauma" was adapted from Will Hall's flyer with the same name.

Psych First Aid Training—Occupy 2011, by North Star Health Collective (originally developed for RNC protests in 2008).

And a very special thanks to everyone involved on the lists.mayfirst.org/mailman/listinfo/occupymentalhealth for your participation, support, and encouragement.

Occupy Mental Health Project: Aki Imai, batushkad, Becca Shaw Glaser, benjahwbc, bob, bryhresboyz, Cal Moen, carolt, crystal.hatfield, Danielle Demos, dashcom, emiko_yo, Eric Stiens, fuerzagoddess, Gaije, gbacque, ginajanwatson, glwrnr, harjitgill, jase.anton, Jonah Bossewitch, josuecardona, lisabfreedman, malainajean, Maryse Mitchell-Brody, M. Osborn, Mind(ful) Liberation Project, mj.allen. newcomb, David Oaks, Rachel Anderson, Rachel Liebert, raheluisa, reesedobbins, reysapo, robinsmurov, Sarah Harper (rockharp@gmail. com, www.myspace.com/rockharper), sandra, Sascha DuBrul, ssoldz, tbranelli, thatsjodi, theodor.arnason, trissypissy, willisa

Collaborative Editing Platform: www.booki.cc

Hosting: Mayfirst.org

Resource List

Freedom Center **www.freedom-center.org**

Harm Reduction Coalition **www.harmreduction.org**

MIND UK **www.mind.org.uk**

Hearing Voices Network **www.hearing-voices.org**

Law Project for Psychiatric Rights **www.psychrights.org**

The Icarus Project **www.theicarusproject.net**

www.activist-trauma.net

Navigating the Space Between Brilliance and Madness

Harm Reduction Guide To Coming off Psychiatric Medications

Friends Make The Best Medicine Support Manual Draft

Promo flyer for the Harm Reduction Guide, with ordering instructions. **theicarusproject.net/files/IcarusNavigatingCrisisHandoutLarge05-09. pdf**

theicarusproject.net/articles/activism-depression

Rock Dove Collective **www.rockdovecollective.org**

Life After Labels **www.lifeafterlabels.org**

psychOUT **psyout.tumblr.com**

Communities Magazine Articles on Mental Health **communities.ic.org/issues/150/Mental_Health_Challenges_and_Hope**

Iraq Veterans Against the War **www.ivaw.org/blog/service-members-have-right-heal, www.ivaw.org/resources/ptsd**

National Center for PTSD **www.ptsd.va.gov**

Vets4Vets—Free Peer Support for Iraq/Afghanistan-Era Vets **www.vets4vets.us**

Safe Helpline 24/7 confidential hotline (assistance for victims of military sexual trauma) **877-995-5247**

Peer Support Crisis Line **804-631-3134**—24/7 confidential and anonymous hot/warmline. Entirely volunteer run, no professionals, no calling the police or forced hospitalization. Just peer support, now.

National Suicide Prevention Hotline **800-273-8255**

Street Medic Wiki **medic.wikia.com/wiki/Main_Page**

Starhawk's Resources for Activism Trainers (including medical/civil disobediance/consensus/understanding oppression resources, etc.) **www.starhawk.org/activism/trainer-resources/trainer-resources.html**

Shields,Katrina (2011) StressManagement and Burnout Prevention, ACLU, **action.aclu.org/site/PageServer?pagename=AS_burnoutprevention**

Participating in Direct Actions: A Guide for Transgender People **srlp.org/resources/publications/participating-direct-actions-guide-transgender-people**

Nonviolent Communication **www.cnvc.org**

Transformative Mediation **www.transformativemediation.org**

Wollman, Neil (2007) Dealing With or Preventing Burnout in Activist Work **www.radpsynet.org/docs/wollman-burnout.html**

Books

firewalkers: madness, beauty & mystery—radically rethinking mental illness, VOCAL, 2009. **thefirebook.org**

Live Through This: On Creativity and Self-Destruction. New York: Seven Stories Press, 2008.

101 Alternatives to Suicide for Teens, Freaks & Other Outlaws. Bornstein, Kate. New York: Seven Stories Press, 2006.

In the Tiger's Mouth: An Empowerment Guide For Social Action. Shields, Katrina (1991) Millenium Books, Newtown, NSW.

About Consent

Beginner's Guide to Responsible Sexuality **www.phillyspissed.net/node/30**

Example Consent Policies from Medic Wiki **medic.wikia.com/wiki/Example_Consent_Policies**

About Sexual Assault, and Activist Communities Responding to Sexual Assault

Rape, Abuse, and Incest National Network **www.rainn.org**

Soul Speak Out: Share your Survivor Story **www.soulspeakout.org**

Dealing with Sexual Assault in Activist Communities from the Northeast Anarchist Network **neanarchist.net/sexual-assault-resources**

Support New York: A Direct Action Survivor Support Network **supportny.org**

Philly Stands Up **phillystandsup.wordpress.com**

Occupy Sites

Occupy Winter **www.facebook.com/OccupyWinterSurvival**

Occupy Patriarchy **www.facebook.com/occupypatriarchy**

Occupy Normal **www.mindfreedom.org/campaign/boycott-normal/
occupy**

Occupy at Home (grassroots movement of people with chronic illness, disabilities, as well as other people with reasons unable to attend Occupies in "meatspace") **occupyathome.wordpress.com**

Occupy on Wheels **www.facebook.com/pages/Occupy-On-Wheels-Awareness-Inclusion-Solidarity**

Occupy Disabled **www.facebook.com/pages/Occupy-Disabled**

Occupy Mental Health/Psychiatry **www.facebook.com/pages/Occupy-Mental-HealthOccupy-Psychiatry**

Occupy Together (list of global Occupy groups) **www.occupytogether.org**